The Carousel Capital of the World

Felicity Fox

The Carousel Capital of the World

Felicity Fox

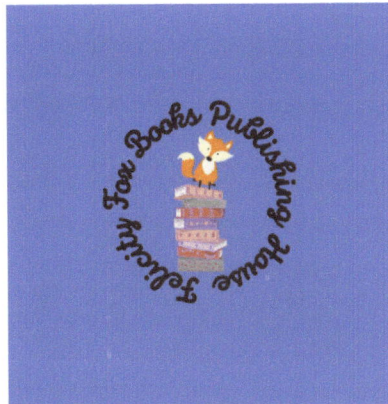

Identifiers:
ISBN Paperback: 978-1-961993-15-0
ISBN Hardcover: 978-1-961993-16-7
ISBN Ebook: 978-1-961993-17-4
LCCN: 2024904150

Preface

In 2013, my three-year-old son and my neighbor's grandson played with toy trucks while we chatted happily over hot tea. A casual conversation about work and life began. My neighbor (K.F.) hadn't known the extent of what I did for a living, so imagine my joy when a few days later, she connected me with a friend of hers (M.J.). M.J. happened to mention that the Endicott Visitor Center was looking for local "talent" to display, which led me to meet the lovely ladies of the Endicott Visitor Center, C.B. in particular. When they hosted me for a book signing for my first book, they mentioned no carousel books were out there that spoke of the incredible history, the reason behind the name: "The Carousel Capital of the World," and what it all represented. So, I took the challenge, and with the use of flyers about the carousels, I penned a story. It's been years in the making, but I hope that rhyming helps to tell the story in a way that is easy to understand. Of course, I weaved in some fantasy, too, because why not?

See the back content on this book for the six carousel locations!

So please enjoy this story, ride the carousel circuit, get your pin, and enjoy the wonderful parks that the EJ founders provided for the community. What blessings they remain!

With Sincere Gratitude,

Felicity

The Greater Binghamton area claimed its fame,
when "The Carousel Capital of the World" became its name.
Within the borders of Canada and the United States,
fewer than 170 carousels remain to date.
The Greater Binghamton area is home to six carousels,
each spinning with colorful horses and stories to tell.

To carefully maintain six spheres of enchantment,
care is taken to preserve each's charm, for enhancement.
The six carousels are considered remarkable spaces
—all are on the National Register of Historic Places.
Most merry-go-rounds have three horses galloping side-by-side,
but three of the carousels keep four in a row prancing with pride.

George F. Johnson donated the six brilliant works of art.

He wanted them to always be enjoyed and never too far apart.

His idea was that each should contribute to a child's happy life,

so he willed youngsters to ride free to keep them from strife.

All are open Memorial through Labor Day within local parks.

The carousels are part of summer fun, adventures, and larks.

ENDICOTT-JOHNSON WORKERS - TANNERS AND SHOE MAKERS

The Endicott Johnson Shoe Company was once quite prominent.

Known as EJ's, it was a local business that was always dominant.

Despite closing its tanneries way back in 1968,

its legacy still lives on due to a corporate great.

George F. Johnson was a great benefactor to EJ's,

an esteemed corporate leader who believed in family ways.

Built by the Allan Herschell Company with precision,
the horses' chariots, saddles, and harnesses are a great vision.
Ross Park and Recreation Park's organs still play a familiar tune:
The Wurlitzer Military Band's music loops each morning and afternoon.
Located on shared grounds with pools, fields, and playgrounds,
splashing water and kids laughing add to the glorious sounds.

CFJ Parks holds the largest carousel that exists, installed in 1923.
It is located in Johnson City and has 72 figures to see.
Also open a few weekends between Thanksgiving and Christmas,
this carousel offers visits with Santa to fulfill your holiday wish.
Decorated with Christmas lights for seasonal carousel rides,
to gallop on four horses abreast, families come from miles wide.

The George W. Johnson Carousel arrived in 1934,
with 36 horses and two chariots to adore.
Located on Oak Hill Avenue on Endicott's northside,
this carousel also awakens for Santa's visits and Christmas rides.
Other Christmas characters have also come for a visit or two.
One year, the Grinch slinked along without the Whoville Who's.

On special holidays and occasions, riders fill up the seats,
especially when a carousel is open for Halloween rides and sweets.
For Christmas, a trolley ride between merry-go-rounds is a treat;
passengers sip hot cocoa while singing carols ever so sweet.
These wonders bring holiday joy to friends and each loved one.
With so much to do and see, the Christmas season has then begun.

Binghamton Zoo
at Ross Park

Zoo Entrance	↑
Parking Ⓐ Ⓑ	↑
Education Ctr	↑
Lion's Den	↑
Carousel	

In 1929, West Endicott's carousel was delivered to its grounds;
a pig and a dog joined the 36 horses that circle around.
In 1920, Ross Park's sphere first spun to the original organ's sound.
On Morgan Road in Binghamton, four horses side by side are found.
Sixty spectacular horses and a zoo all live here,
plus two chariots, one with monkeys, are all in the sphere.

Highland
Park
Endwell

George W.
Johnson Park
Endicott

West
Endicott
Park
Endicott

C. Fred Johnson Park
Johnson City

Recreation Park
Binghamton

Ross Park
Binghamton

79

26

81

88

52

41

17/86

81

17/86

117

79

Recreation Park received its carousel in 1925,
with sixty horses, four abreast, its original music still thrives.
In 1925, a carousel came to En-Joie Park for a short reign.
In 1966, it relocated to Highland Park in Endwell where it remains.
A pig and a dog joined 36 horses in Highland's circle of fun.
It's a sixth wonder that families enjoy until the day is done.

Paying a visit to all six merry-go-rounds is a win.

As all are welcome to "ride the circuit" and to receive a pin.

The horses appear in "country fair" style on each sphere,

with bright, almond-shaped eyes set close to their ears.

Saddle blankets made with animal pelts and glass jewels are not shoddy.

With round dish saddles and short legs drawn close to each horse's body.

SCHOOL

George F. Johnson Elementary

CFJ Park is named after Charles F. Johnson.

He was the older brother, by two years, of George F. Johnson.

George W. was George F's son, whose name remains—

The park on Oak Hill Ave. was given his name.

Schools, structures, and libraries all carry on the legacy,

with the Johnson family and other EJ partners' names etched so splendidly.

NICE

1. Aaron
2. Madison
3. Sydney
4. Alexis
5. Harrison
6. Harley

Carousel horses are jumpers, as seen by their up and down motion,
and because they jump at the chance to help with Santa's locomotion.
You see, the horses do not lay dormant from September to May.
On the contrary, they are busy helping to navigate Santa's sleigh.
Santa keeps his nice list handy for his toy drops.
The jumpers steer the reindeer toward the right kids' rooftops.

When the horses were positioned and painting first began,
magic sparkled as the horses first took flight and then ran.
Though completely invisible to the human eye,
their golden wings carry them galloping through the sky.
Each carousel has one solid-colored mare known as the lead horse.
A nod of her head and ease of her tail awakens a magic force.

As they soar, each horse's wings illuminate the stars.
Zipping through the night sky, they travel near and far.
At speeds too fast for the human eye to clearly decipher,
They're shooting stars filling the sky like light-filled geysers.
Since they can fly through the sky without detection and with ease,
gallivanting with other carousel jumpers is a breeze.

When you blink, that is when they fly as they please.

The jumpers flawlessly slip back into their places with complete ease.

Echoes of a carousel full of children giggling together

create precious, wholesome memories to treasure forever.

These wonders bring laughter and pure joy to friends and loved ones.

Within these magical moments is genuine, timeless, and endless fun.

Inlaid with intricate details, the carousels are stunning works of art.

In the Greater Binghamton area, they are dear to the city's heart.

Flawless and full of adventures within the sphere,

they have something to offer visitors from far or near.

Sprinkled with magic for spontaneous escapades,

they create laughter, smiles, and friendships, as memories are made.

Where to Find the Six Carousels That Represent the Carousel Capital of the World

CFJ CAROUSEL
98 C.F.J. Boulevard, Johnson City, NY 13790
(607) 797-3031
svillageofjohn@stny.rr.com
(607) 797-3031

RECREATION PARK CAROUSEL
58-78 Beethoven Street, Binghamton, NY 13901
(607) 772-7017
jabrigham@cityofbinghamton.com
(607) 772-7017

GEORGE W. JOHNSON PARK CAROUSEL
201 Oak Hill Avenue, Endicott, NY 13760
(607) 757-2461
mayorsec@endicottny.com
(607) 757-2461

ROSS PARK CAROUSEL
60 Morgan Road, Binghamton, NY 13903
(607) 772-7017
jabrigham@cityofbinghamton.com
(607) 772-7017

HIGHLAND PARK CAROUSEL
801 Hooper Road, Endwell, NY 13760
(607) 786-2970
parks@townofunion.com
(607) 786-2970

WEST ENDICOTT PARK CAROUSEL
525 Maple Street (at Page Avenue), Endicott, NY 13760
(607) 786-2970
parks@townofunion.com
(607) 786-2970

Check out Felicity's website
for all your editing and
publishing needs.

www.thefelicityfoxhouse.com

www.ingramcontent.com/pod-product-compliance
Lightning Source LLC
Chambersburg PA
CBHW060803270326
41926CB00002B/72